CIM REVISION CARDS

Strategic Marketing Decisi

Mike Willoughby of Marketing Knowledge

AMSTERDAM • BOSTON • HEIDELBERG • LONDON • NEW YORK • OXFORD
PARIS • SAN DIEGO • SAN FRANCISCO • SINGAPORE • SYDNEY • TOKYO

Butterworth-Heinemann is an imprint of Elsevier

ELSEVIER

Butterworth-Heinemann is an imprint of Elsevier
Linacre House, Jordan Hill, Oxford OX2 8DP
30 Corporate Drive, Suite 400, Burlington, MA 01803

First published 2008

Permissions may be sought directly from Elsevier's Science & Technology Rights Department in Oxford, UK: phone: (+44) (0) 1865 843830; fax: (+44) (0) 1865 853333,
e-mail: permissions @ elsevier.co.uk. You may also complete your request on-line via the Elsevier homepage
(http://www.elsevier.com), by selecting 'Customer Support' and then 'Obtaining Permissions'.

British Library Cataloguing in Publication Data
A catalogue record for this book is available from the British Library

ISBN-13: 978-0-7506-8655-6

For information on all Butterworth-Heinemann publications visit our web site at http://books.elsevier.com

Printed and bound in Spain

08 09 10   10 9 8 7 6 5 4 3 2 1

TABLE OF CONTENTS

PREFACE

Welcome to the CIM Revision Cards from Elsevier/Butterworth–Heinemann. We hope you will find these useful to revise for your CIM exam. The cards are designed to be used in conjunction with the CIM Coursebooks from Elsevier/Butterworth–Heinemann, and have been written specifically with revision in mind. They also serve as invaluable reviews of the complete modules, perfect for those studying via the assignment route.

■ Learning outcomes at the start of each chapter identify the main points

■ Key topics are summarised, helping you commit the information to memory quickly and easily

■ Examination and revision tips are provided to give extra guidance when preparing for the exam

■ Key diagrams are featured to aid the learning process

■ The compact size ensures the cards are easily transportable, so you can revise any time, anywhere.

To get the most of your revision cards, try to look over them as frequently as you can when taking your CIM course. When read alongside the Coursebook they serve as the ideal companion to the main text. Good luck – we wish you every success with your CIM qualification!

INTRODUCTION TO STRATEGIC MARKETING DECISIONS

Unit 1

1.1 Examine the role of life cycles in strategic decisions to manage competitive advantage across global, international and domestic markets.

1.2 Examine the influence of market position on strategy and performance.

1.3 Critically appraise the changing dimensions of strategic decisions made to sustain competitive advantage in today's global markets.

1.4 Assess how product/market/brand/customer life cycles can be managed strategically across markets.

1.5 Examine the role of competitive relationships and how organizations compete to achieve customer preference.

Syllabus References: 1.1–1.5

KEY DEFINITIONS

A stakeholder – is anyone who has an interest in or an impact on an organization's activities.

Strategic marketing decisions – are the decisions made as part of the iterative process of strategy development. A company makes these decisions in response to the changing dimensions of the marketing environment in order to ensure a sustainable competitive advantage. Strategic marketing decisions are part of the problem-solving process and are required throughout the process of analysis, strategic choice and implementation.

A sustainable competitive advantage – is the achievement of a company to develop a superior, differentiated position in the market place which creates superior value for customers, shareholders and stakeholders and which they are able to maintain over a period of time.

Hard-edged marketing – is the process by which marketing managers ensure they make decisions that create superior value for all stakeholders, especially customers and shareholders, and prove the value of marketing's contribution to business by the use of meaningful marketing metrics.

Market/competitive lifecycles – describe the cyclical nature of the demand and competitive activity in markets. Lifecycles are based on the notion that during the life time of a market, it passes through a number of distinct phases, each of which has particular characteristics with regard to the nature of competitor activity, the demand for a product and the type of strategies that are appropriate to meet the distinct characteristics of the phase.

The evolution of marketing thinking

From a long-term perspective, marketing has developed through four stages of thinking. Taking a shorter term view, marketing managers and decision makers have to respond to five priorities.

<table>
<tr><td>

Stages of marketing thinking (Doyle, 2000)

■ Transactional Marketing – focusing on short term profits

■ Brand Marketing – building customer loyalty by building an attachment, emotional or otherwise, between the customer and the brand

■ Relationship marketing – building customer loyalty and retention through a wider range of approaches with an emphasis on retention

■ Value-based marketing – building value to shareholders by delivering a total value proposition to an organization's customers

</td><td>

Five priorities for decision makers (Wilson and Gilligan, 2004)

■ The pace of change and need to respond with innovative solutions

■ Fragmented markets and the increased need to customise

■ Superior customer value as a basic ingredient of competitiveness

■ Information, market knowledge and the ability to learn as a source of competitive advantage

■ The strategic significance of new types of partnerships and new networks of relationships in the supply chain

</td></tr>
</table>

The changing dimensions of competitive advantage – the role of lifecycles

The bases of competitive advantage are continually changing as the environment changes. These changes are influenced by a number of lifecycles, which will vary across the world. This variance poses both an opportunity and a challenge for strategic decision makers.

The Market/Industry Lifecycle has four distinct stages moving from new firms and little concentration through emergence of competition, specialisation, and, finally, to consolidation and withdrawal of all but the strongest players.

Demand/Technology Lifecycles consist of the demand lifecycle which is the underlying need within the market whilst the technology lifecycle deals with the ways in which this need is satisfied.

The Competitive Lifecycle dictates that pioneers who achieve first mover advantage are challenged by competitors, leading to a diminishing opportunity for premium pricing and, ultimately, commodity competition.

How organizations compete to achieve customer preference

Treacy and Wieresma (1995) propose four focuses by which companies may achieve customer preferences:

Operational Excellence – Companies compete not by technological innovation but by targeting a customer preference for value for money

Customer Intimacy – Companies can target on an individual basis through mass customisation of both products and marketing

Product Leadership – Companies focus on developing products that push at the boundaries of innovation, making high investments in research and development

Brand Leadership – Companies base their strategic position on brand leadership supported by the extra value proposition created by the brand

The role of competitive relationships

An integral part of many companies' strategy is to form relationships with competitors in order to achieve sustainable competitive advantage. The driving forces for this trend are as follows:

- Companies do not have **sufficient resources** alone to realise their full global potential and so may form a relationship to achieve better operational excellence or perhaps greater customer intimacy.
- The **pace of innovation and market diffusion** is ever more rapid and so, to achieve global brand leadership, relationships may be formed so that new products and services can be exploited quickly by effective diffusion into the global market.
- **High R&D costs** mean it is increasingly difficult, costly and risky for companies to develop breakthrough innovations alone. Thus to achieve product leadership, relationships may be formed in R&D as in the Sony/Philips alliance, which produced the new mini disc player.
- In **mature markets** such as the car and airline industries operational excellence has been achieved by the formation of alliances, mergers and takeovers to rationalise competition, achieve economies of scale and so achieve cost leadership in the industry.
- Some companies use relationships to acquire the capability **to access new markets** where they have little expertise or experience so they are better positioned to compete for customer preference in those markets.

Revision tips

■ It is important to understand the way in which lifecycles develop across the world, leading to differing conditions in different countries and regions. These lead to differing critical success factors for these markets and so differing bases of competitive advantage being required of the successful players. These are continually changing as the lifecycles continue to develop.

■ In order to avoid strategic drift, organizations have to take account of the changing critical success factors and bases of competitive advantage and review and develop their strategies accordingly.

■ Finally, Strategic Marketing Decisions need to be made and implemented – this implementation itself requiring a carefully designed project plan with clear objectives and management skills appropriate to the project.

CHALLENGING TRADITIONAL STRATEGIC THINKING

Unit 2

Traditional strategic thinking

There are two interpretations of this phrase, both of which are valid to consider:

1. **Traditional thinking within organizations**. 'This is the way we have always done things'. As markets and economies move through their lifecycles, the bases of competitive advantage are likely to change. Organizations have, therefore, to consider how they should respond.

2. **Traditional methods of developing strategy**. As the pace of change increases so a premium is put on the ability of organizations to adapt to change. Approaches that are more organic and flexible than traditional linear approaches have, therefore, to be considered.

Breakpoints – Occur in markets as a consequence of a major change in the environment or the competitive nature of the market which results in a previously successful strategy being made obsolete.

Value-based marketing – A marketing strategy that is based on a totally integrated marketing effort which delivers superior value to customers and so in turn delivers superior value to shareholders.

Shareholder value principle – The shareholder value principle asserts that marketing strategies should be judged by the economic returns they generate for shareholders, the returns being measured by dividends and increases in the company share price.

Emergent strategies – A strategy that has been developed through an iterative learning process so that the resultant strategy is one that has emerged through the creative and iterative process of crafting a strategy of proactively seeking new opportunities whilst reacting to the challenges faced in the market.

Drivers for realignment in strategic thinking

Four emergent needs drive strategic alignment. These are:

Emergent needs
- Rising customer expectations
- The drive for increased revenue and growth from the marketplace
- The intensification of global competition
- The need for innovation and creativity

The following environmental factors give rise to these:

Issues/environmental factors
- Increasing globalisation of the marketplace
- Emergence of the global village
- Growth and movement of populations across the globe
- Growing body of international law
- Piracy
- Shrinking communications
- The Internet and access to the world wide web

Application of new marketing thinking to strategic decisions

The need for innovative thinking

Wilson and Gilligan (2004) suggest that changes in the marketing environment create breakpoints for the following reasons:

- Changes in demographics or social structure
- Technological breakthroughs
- The identification of new business opportunities which redefine the market
- Shifts within the distribution network leading to changes in power balances and consequent changes in expectations
- Indirect competitors becoming direct competitors by developing new capabilities
- Maturity of markets forcing rethinks in the face of declining returns.

Piercy (2002), states that this leads to the need for strategic decisions to be concerned with:

- How to create value
- How to harness the power and impact of the Internet, particularly in relation to channel decisions
- How to achieve a totally integrated marketing effort to create customer value
- How to engender creativity within an organization and avoid the bureaucracy associated with formal planning

Application of new marketing thinking to strategic decisions

The need to deliver shareholder value

Doyle (2000) suggests that,

The key to creating shareholder value is building relationships with target customers based on satisfying their needs more effectively than competitors

■ The shareholder value principle asserts that marketing strategies should be judged by the increase in value that they generate for the company based on the net present value of the income and expenditure streams together with the change in value of the company. Two principles then apply:

◇ The primary obligation of managers is to maximise returns for shareholders and owners

◇ The stock market value of a company (the market capitalisation) is based on the investors' expectations of the cash generating abilities of the company.

Doyle further states that delivering Value-Based Marketing requires the following:

■ A deep understanding of customer needs, operating procedures and decision-making processes

■ The formulation of value propositions that create differential advantage in meeting these needs

■ Building long-term relationships with customers based on satisfaction and confidence in the supplier

■ An understanding that the delivery of superior value is based on superior knowledge, systems, skills and marketing assets.

Alternative approaches to strategic marketing decisions

There are clear differences between the rational formal approach and the emergent strategy approach to decision making.

Rational Formal Approach

- Linear formal approach
- Hierarchical structure of decisions
- Use of models and planning frameworks
- Distinct steps
- Chief Executive responsible for whole process whilst operational managers are separately responsible for implementation
- Strategies are detailed and explicit

Emergent Strategy Approach

- Development of strategy is an iterative process
- Decisions are smaller and may be taken anywhere in the organization
- These small decisions take shape until they form an articulated strategy
- This approach implies both the empowerment and the ability to undertake systematic analysis throughout the organization

Strategic decision making in SMEs

Small and Medium sized Enterprises (SMEs) have particular issues and, therefore, adopt appropriate responses.

Issues
- Limited resources:
  - ◇ Time
  - ◇ Finance
  - ◇ Professional expertise
- Often no 'team of functional experts'
- The Managing Director may have sole responsibility for Strategic Marketing Decisions

Responses
- Emergent approach to decision making
- Creation of 'Virtual Organizations' by developing a network of relationships
- Relationships:
  - ◇ *Inform* strategy development
  - ◇ *Add form* to the strategy

Revision tips

■ Strategic Decisions are based on developing and leveraging sustainable sources of competitive advantage. These are, however, often affected by changes in the macro or micro environment, including the actions of competitors and the expectations of customers.

■ This unit focuses on the need and reasons for continual review of environmental changes and consequent challenge of extant thinking within an organization.

■ Identify the global and local drivers that affect sources of competitive advantage, together with competitive actions that do the same.

■ Consider how organizations should respond to these changes by developing innovative strategies.

■ This response may be achieved by adopting a less formal approach to planning, allowing emergent strategies to be considered alongside formally planned strategies. This may, of course, require an appropriate change in the culture of the organization.

■ Finally, remember that the ultimate aim of Strategic Decisions is to deliver value to shareholders and, in order to achieve this, must deliver value to other stakeholder groups as well, particularly customers.

COMPETITIVE STRATEGY AS A LEARNING PROCESS

Unit 3

LEARNING OUTCOMES

2.7 Explore competitive marketing strategy as an emergent/learning process.
2.8 Examine the role of knowledge management in sustaining competitive advantage.
2.9 Evaluate the incorporation of customer-led internet marketing into marketing strategies.
3.9 Appreciate the value of effective knowledge management in creating competitive advantage.

Syllabus References: 2.7–2.9, 3.9

Learning and knowledge management

- In order to make effective decisions, managers must have access to information on which to base them. Knowledge must, therefore, be both acquired ('learning') and processed and distributed to those who need it ('managing').

- Information must be acquired, which is not necessarily a learning process in this case, and managed.

KEY DEFINITIONS

Market orientation – The presence of a culture within an organization, which is focused towards the understanding of customer and competitors and so can create superior value for consumers.

Learning organization – An organization that has an effective learning capability and is able to efficiently manage its knowledge base to re-orient strategies and respond to competitive challenges and so reshape themselves to sustain their competitiveness.

Signal learning – Signal learning is concerned with monitoring the environment and the signalling of challenges and changes in a firm's markets and its performance in that market.

3R learning – The 3Rs stand for reflect, re-evaluate and respond. 3R learning occurs in anticipation of, and in response to, critical events occurring in a firm's markets. It is this type of learning that firms that successfully reinvent themselves undergo in reflecting on the demise of their traditional basis for competitive advantage.

Knowledge management – The systematic management of the knowledge gained through rigorous approach to the research and analysis undertaken. To make effective strategic decisions, it is of paramount importance that the knowledge built is trustworthy, credible and verifiable and that it is accessible to all the managers involved in the decision-making process.

Competitive strategy as an emergent learning process

Sustainable competitive advantage is built on the ability to adapt to changing market conditions and so make effective decisions to develop and implement a strategy which delivers superior value to customers. Learning is required to acquire and develop the skills to do this.

Wilson and Gilligan (2004) suggest the following elements of a **customer value-based philosophy**:

- A strong market orientation
- A process of continuous learning
- A commitment to innovation

Organizational values for effective learning

- A commitment to learning
- Open mindedness
- A shared vision
- Organizational knowledge sharing

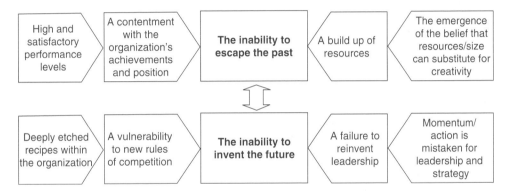

Fig. 3.1. Barriers to escaping from the past and building for the future
Adapted from Hamel and Prahalad (1994)

Knowledge management informing strategy

The macro environment
- Identification of SLEPT factors that affect an organization's environment
- Evaluation of the impact that these factors will have on the organization including buyer behaviour and ability to supply

Industry/market analysis
- Identification of industry and geographical boundaries
- Identification and effect of stakeholders
- Impact of Porter's five Forces on the industry

Competitor analysis
- Identification of current and potential competitors within your present and future markets
- Identification of their strengths, weaknesses and intentions
- Identification of their response patterns to competition

Customer analysis
- Who they are and what they buy
- Who is involved in their decisions
- Why and how do they purchase
- When, where and how often do they purchase

Revision tips

- This unit deals with the ability of organizations to both learn and develop processes to manage that learning and the outcomes from it.

- Ensure, therefore, that you are familiar with types of learning, Signal and 3R (note that different terminology is used by different authors on this topic), the type of information that is required on which to base Strategic Decisions relating to competitive strategies and, finally, the processes and systems that must be put in place to support learning and information management.

- The Internet plays different roles in organizations. In some it is fundamental to their competitive strategy, in other, it has a less important role, possibly simply as a promotional medium. However, even for these organizations, it is important to recognise that competitors may be leveraging its capability more effectively. This is particularly the case where the competitors are smaller and more agile.

- Whilst International Marketing is not treated separately within the syllabus, you should consider the implications of the more complex and uncertain aspects of gathering and managing information on an international or global scale.

DEVELOPING CORPORATE WIDE MARKETING INNOVATION

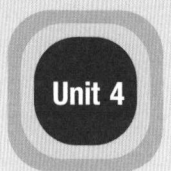
Unit 4

LEARNING OUTCOMES

2.2 Explain the nature of innovation in marketing and the factors affecting its development in decisions to create competitive advantage and customer preference.

2.3 Evaluate the role of innovation management and risk-taking in achieving competitive advantage.

2.4 Examine the issues in creating an innovative marketing culture within an organization.

2.9 Evaluate the incorporation of customer-led Internet marketing into marketing strategies.

Syllabus References: 2.2–2.4, 2.9

The nature and impact of innovation

- In this unit, innovation is examined from a number of perspectives.

- First, the nature of technological innovation is considered, together with the processes necessary to exploit it effectively.

- Following on from this, the implications of bringing new products to market, utilising innovative approaches, including the Internet, are examined.

- Finally, the creation of an organizational culture to facilitate innovation is considered.

Diffusion curve – is the model of the spread of a new product into the markets, split into customer response segments (innovators, early adopters, early majority, late majority and laggards).

Industry breakpoints – are defined (Strebel, 1996) as a new offering to the market that is so superior in terms of customer value that it disrupts the rules of the competitive game. Two types of breakpoints are discussed. *Divergent breakpoints* are associated with the sharply increasing variety in the competitive offerings and consequently higher value for the customer. *Convergent breakpoints* are the result of improvements in the system and processes resulting in lower delivered costs.

Continuous innovations – cause negligible or slightly disruptive effects upon the purchase and consumption of the product.

Dynamically continuous innovations – have a more disruptive effect on the way that the products and services are used.

Discontinuous innovations – have a highly disruptive effect upon usage and purchasing patterns and these innovations require a high level of marketing to explain the benefits and to educate consumers about how the product should be used.

Technology lifecycle and competitive advantage

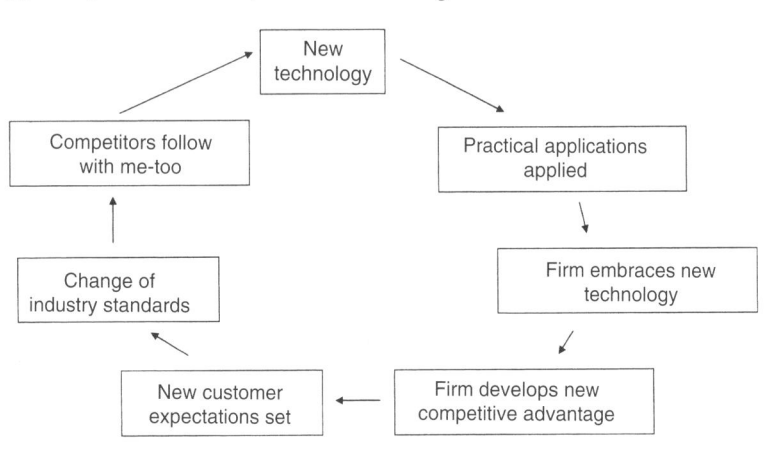

Fig. 4.1.
Source: Doole and Lowe (2005)

Diffusion curve

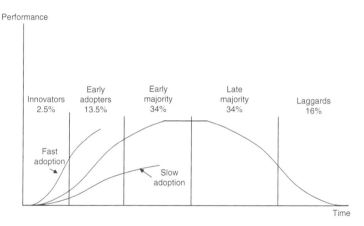

Fig. 4.2.
Source: Adapted from Doole and Lowe: CIM Coursebook *Strategic Marketing Decisions*
(Elsevier Butterworth-Heinemann, 2006)

Opportunity identification

Doole and Lowe (2005) have discussed techniques to identify opportunities. These include the following:

- Scientific exploration – that starts with no immediate application or customer benefit in mind.
- Analysis of current and anticipated customer needs – is an obvious starting point. Asking customers what they want usually identifies new product and service developments.
- Segmenting markets further – than they have been segmented before is an effective way of developing products and services to meet more effectively the needs of subsegments of customers.
- Identifying a new emerging segment – that is born out of changes in the mood, attitudes and expectation of customers and dissatisfaction with current offerings.
- Applying existing techniques in a new sector – applying a technology, process or technique from one business sector to another.
- Vertical integration – of the supply chain creating a new, better value route to market.
- Business rationalisation – or mergers often lead to some products and services being no longer required or a customer segment no longer being satisfied.
- Innovation in mature sectors – Innovations have taken place here by offering customers a quantum leap in value.

The innovation process

In respect of product and service innovation, a systematic process is required to:

■ Increase the number of ideas coming forward
■ Better manage the process from idea generation to commercialisation
■ Increase the chances of success
■ Screen out potential losing ideas as early as possible in order to avoid wasting effort
■ Minimise the early costs of investigating individual ideas
■ Encourage everyone in the organization to suggest innovations and improvements
■ Increase the speed to market
■ Maximise the value of the innovation

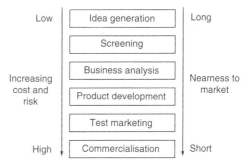

Fig. 4.3.
Source: Doole and Lowe: CIM Coursebook *Strategic Marketing Decisions* (Elsevier Butterworth-Heinemann, 2006).

Marketing strategy process innovations

Table 4.1.

Innovations	Some examples
Environmental changes	Responding to legal changes (e.g. safety or environmental pollution regulations, market derogation)
	Responding to technological advances
Resources and capabilities audit	Exploiting company competencies in a new way (e.g. using e-business)
Strategy	Segmenting the market further than it is at present
	Repositioning to benefit from changes in customer needs and attitudes
Market entry alternatives	Participating in an alliance to redefine the market
The marketing mix	Focusing on interactive rather than mass communications
Supply chain	Finding new value from supply chain contributions
Relationships	Redefining the mix to solution provision, rather than selling products and services

Innovation in internet marketing

Table 4.2.

Six-Is	Characteristics of the Internet
Interactivity	Customer initiated contact
	Marketer has 100% customer attention
Intelligence	Can continuously collect and analyse information and make individually focused offers
Individualisation	Marketing communications is tailored to meet individual needs so achieving mass customisation
Integration	Managing integrated external and internal marketing communications and mixed mode buying
Industry restructuring	Disintermediation involves removing the traditional intermediaries from the distribution channel
	Reintermediation involves gaining a presence on websites that might fulfil the role of intermediary
Independence of location	Reach can be extended into countries where it is not viable to locate a significant sales support activity

Adapted from Deighton (1996)

Revision tips

■ Innovation is a frequent theme of Post-graduate diploma exam questions. Ensure that you are familiar both with the different categories of innovations from 'new to the world breakthroughs' to minor adaptations.

■ As well as being familiar with the processes of innovation, consider the organizational implications of creating an environment that nurtures innovation: processes, resources, reward systems and organizational attitude and culture.

■ Remember that innovation extends to embrace far more than simply products and services. Innovative approaches to marketing strategy applied to both new and existing products and services can deliver enhanced value to an organization.

■ Finally ensure that you are familiar with the ways in which the Internet can affect the whole of an organization's innovation strategy, from facilitating the gathering of information, through adding value to product to new distribution and promotional approaches.

DEVELOPING CORPORATE WIDE MARKETING INNOVATION

Unit 5

Evaluating and developing strategy

- In the face of a continually changing environment in which the bases of competitive advantage are not only changing with time, but also vary across markets which have differing lifecycles, organizations must make positive decisions to avoid strategic drift.

- These decisions will rest on adopting generic competitive and targeting & positioning strategies that are appropriate both to the market. opportunities and to the organization's competitive stance or market position (e.g. Leader, Challenger, Follower and so on).

KEY DEFINITIONS

Five definitions of strategy

Strategies can be intended

1. **Strategy as a plan** – a consciously intended course of action.

2. **Strategy as a play** – just a specific manoeuvre to outwit rivals.

Strategies can be realised through behaviour

3. **Strategy as a pattern** – a stream of consistent behaviours, whether intended or not. It is worth comparing strategic intent with strategic reality. Strategic intent is often only partially realised in the form of a delivered strategy (the reality). There is often an unrealised part of this strategy, which leaves gaps that are often filled by emergent strategies that are not part of the initial intentions.

Strategy can be about external focus

4. **Strategy as a position** – a unique location for the organization within its environment achieved by matching up the organization (internal context) with the environment (external context).

Strategy can also be an internal focus

5. **Strategy as a perspective** – an ingrained way of perceiving the world.

Source: Mintzberg *et al.*, 2003

Strategy evaluation: the reasons for marketing strategy failure and wear-out

- Poor general management and inability to implement an appropriate strategy:
  - Operational inefficiency
  - Lack of investment
  - Poor leadership
- An inability to cope with market changes:
  - Economic and sector lifecycles
  - Legislative and technological changes
  - Slower than expected growth or diffusion
  - Distribution channels

- Ineffective marketing management:
  - Ineffective use of marketing tools and resources
  - Emergence of competitive innovation or new competitors
  - Overdependence on one customer or product
- Removal of a protected environment:
  - End of a monopoly
  - Change of customer needs
  - Lack of customer and competitor focus

Alternative marketing approaches

Product push marketing – is an approach that concentrates on persuading customers to buy the products and services that the firm can produce, deliver and further develop easily, largely using their existing realm of knowledge and resources.

Customer-led marketing – is typified by those organizations that do everything they can to satisfy customer needs. Some organizations have taken this to extremes and set out to deliver customer needs almost irrespective of cost.

Resource-based marketing – is considered to be a balanced strategy between meeting the market requirements and exploiting the organization's capabilities to serve the market. Resource-based marketing takes into account the competitive situation, the full range of assets, skills and competencies of the organization and aims to exploit the organization's role within the supply chain.

Entrepreneurial marketing – Entrepreneurs tend to focus on the opportunity or market gap, irrespective of whether or not this will make use of existing assets and resources. Entrepreneurial marketing usually takes the form of a new business start or a new spin out from within an existing firm.

Network marketing – is becoming increasingly significant as organizations, desperate for growth, use connections through alliances, partnerships and equity participation in other organizations to exploit opportunities that are not deliverable through their directly owned assets.

Criteria for a successful strategy

Adapted from Mintzberg *et al.* (2003)

- Clear decisive objectives: although subordinate goals may change in the heat of the campaign or competition, the overriding goals must remain clear and understood.

- Maintaining the initiative: it must allow freedom of action, enhance commitment and maintain the pace and determine the course of events, rather than reacting to them.

- Concentration: it must be capable of concentrating superior power at a particular place and time to be decisive.

- Flexibility: it must keep in reserve resources and capabilities in order to allow flexibility and manoeuvrability.

- Co-ordinated and committed leadership: leaders must be appointed for each of the goals, and their interests and ambitions must match the needs of their roles.

- Surprise: it must make use of speed, secrecy and intelligence to attack unprepared competitors.

- Security: it must secure resources to support the actions.

Competitive stances

The first three categories are discussed by Wilson and Gilligan under the terminology of competitive position; Doole and Lowe add two further categories of Pioneers and Market Nichers:

Leaders – keep ahead of the field by developing an ever-stronger selling proposition and competitive advantage to build customer loyalty, discouraging other possible market entrants.

Challengers – develop a strong alternative proposition and challenge the leader's weaknesses continually, often by aggressive pricing.

Followers – imitate the other competitors at lower prices. They look for unexploited opportunities.

Pioneers – innovators who tend to be first into new opportunities. Some may also be market leaders but others may not maintain a consistent strategy and may fail to consolidate their pioneering efforts and build their businesses.

Market Nichers – survive and grow through specialising in a part of the market that is too small to be attractive to larger firms or in a market niche that they define and create themselves. With globalisation some market nichers have built substantial businesses through creating a global niche.

Revision tips

- The redefinition of strategy is central to this module and it is vital to exam success to understand clearly the fundamentals of this area. Ansoff's corporate growth strategies remain an important area to understand clearly.

- Opportunities in each market segment should be matched against the assets and competencies of the organization and prioritised by the suitability of the strategic fit to achieving the organization's objectives.

- In doing so, a number of factors should be considered, including the generic basis of competition in that segment (Cost Leadership, Focus or Differentiation) and Competitive Stance. The latter, especially, is a recurring theme in CIM Postgraduate examinations.

- Strategies may then be tested against other criteria, including acceptability to stakeholders, feasibility and sustainability.

- A suitable positioning for each targeted segment may then be developed and implemented.

- Alternative approaches to developing strategies, planned or emergent, are appropriate to different types of organization. In these cases, the organizations must nurture the capability to develop strategies using these approaches and must ensure that processes, skills and knowledge are managed appropriately at relevant levels within the organization.

STRATEGIC DECISIONS FOR GLOBAL DEVELOPMENT

Unit 6

LEARNING OUTCOMES

3.1 Examine the issues of decisions to build competitive capability and approaches to leveraging capability to create advantage across geographically diverse markets.

3.6 Determine the lessons of best practice from strategic decisions made by successful global companies.

3.10 Leverage individual and corporate learning across geographically diverse markets for competitive advantage.

Syllabus References: 3.1, 3.6, 3.10

International and global marketing

There are two major differences between national and international/global marketing:

■ Self-evidently, international marketing is inherently **more complex** than national marketing. Not only are there more variables to manage, the level of uncertainty may be higher as information is less reliable.

■ Although the vast majority of organizations are involved in international marketing because they face international competition, the **extent of internationalisation of their own operations** is within their own control and, is, therefore, a strategic decision that organizations have to make.

■ ■ ■ ■ ■ ■ ■ ■ ■ ■ ■ ■ ■ ■ ■ ■ ■ ■

■ ■ ■ ■ ■ ■ ■ ■ ■ ■ ■ ■ ■ ■ ■

KEY DEFINITIONS

Export marketing – The marketing of goods and/
or services across national/political boundaries.

Multinational marketing – The marketing
activities of an organization which has activities,
interests or operations in more than one country
and where there is some kind of influence of
control of marketing activities from outside the
country in which the goods or services will actually
be sold, but where the global markets are primarily
perceived to be independent markets and profit
centres in their own right.

Global marketing – Where the whole organization
focuses on the selection and exploitation of global
marketing opportunities and marshals resources
around the globe with the objective of achieving a
global competitive advantage.

Drivers of globalisation

- **Increased market access** as markets in China, Central and Eastern Europe are opened up
- **Increased market opportunities** because of the deregulation of many markets
- **Greater uniformity of industry standards**, encouraged, for example, by the EU Sourcing of products and services from a wider range of countries, particularly those emerging markets with a high ratio of skills to cost
- **More globally standardised products and services**
- **Common technology** used in many more markets, particularly markets where there is a high cost of R&D that must be recovered through sales in many countries
- Similar customer requirements leading to **transnational customer segments**
- Competition from the same organizations in each major market and thus **interdependence of markets**
- **Cooperation between organizations** from different parts of the world, leading to companies competing and cooperating with each other in the same markets
- Worldwide or regional **organization of distribution**, ignoring country boundaries
- **Communication** generated and received almost anywhere in the world
- Global organization strategies that increasingly treat the world as **one market**.

Strategy alternatives for global firms

Alternative worldwide strategies

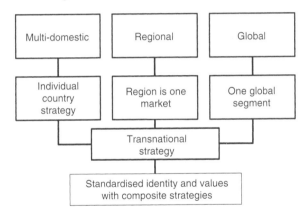

Fig. 6.1.
Source: Doole and Lowe (2004)

Leveraging capability in global markets

The **benefits for a firm** are increasing its scale of operations through increased global activity. They include:

- Better knowledge of the requirements and expectations of customers worldwide

- The economies associated with increased scale of operations and R&D

- Improving efficiency and effectiveness through repeating programmes and processes and, as a result...

- Building the capability and knowledge of the organization that can be applied to new business and marketing initiatives.

These benefits are best achieved through **Programme and Process Standardisation**. Note, however:

- The standardisation of programmes will achieve the benefit of lower costs

- Standardisation of programmes may not be advisable because of differences in market conditions and culture. Organizations should, therefore, decide on the degree of programme standardisation that is appropriate

- Standardisation of processes is more desirable because it not only enables savings to be made but also facilitates corporate learning.

International marketing challenges

Firms face a number of critical strategic decisions and issues of implementation in achieving best practice in International Marketing:

Opportunity analysis and marketing research – are essential to decide which countries are most commercially attractive, offer the most potential and can most effectively be served by the company.

Sensitivity to different cultures – is essential throughout the process, including customer research, product and service development, and communications.

Transnational segmentation – Over-focus on country characteristics segmentation rather than transnational benefit segmentation can seriously curtail global development because of the failure to benefit from scale economies. Good practice requires a hierarchy approach starting with transnational segmentation followed then by country-based segmentation.

Market entry strategies – Arguably the most critical decision for organizations is deciding which market entry strategy to adopt. A balance has to be struck between host market involvement & control and the level of involvement & risk.

Marketing mix – There are a series of decisions about the marketing mix, the level of standardisation that is possible and adaptation to local market needs that is necessary. Decisions are required on the product portfolio, new product development, distribution, communications and pricing strategy and each of these are critical. Decisions are influenced by different factors, including the stage of economic development, cultural demands, legal controls, usage conditions and ethical considerations.

The geographic development of SMEs

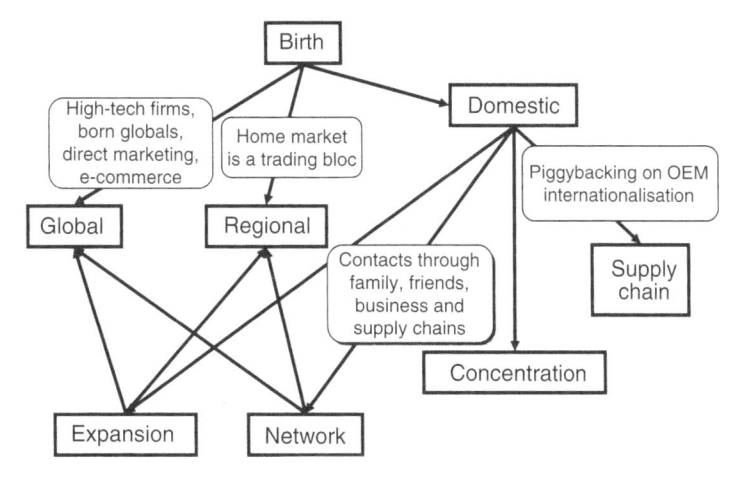

Fig. 6.2.
Source: Doole and Lowe: CIM Coursebook *Strategic Marketing Decisions* (Elsevier Butterworth-Heinemann, 2006)

The importance of niche marketing

Difference between exporting and niche marketing

Table 6.1

	Exporting	International niche marketing
Marketing strategy	Selling production capacity	Meeting customer needs
Financial objective	To amortise overheads	To add value
Segmentation	Usually by country and customer characteristics	By identifying common international customer benefit
Pricing	Cost based	Market or customer based
Management focus	Efficiency in operations	Meeting market requirements
Distribution	Using existing agents or distributors	Managing the supply chain
Market information	Relying on agent or distributor feedback	Analysing the market situation and customer needs
Customer relationship	Working through intermediaries	Building multiple level relationships

Source: Doole and Lowe (2004)

Leveraging learning in SMEs

Levels of internationalisation

SMEs can be characterised by their proactivity in international marketing and can be categorised as passive, reactive, experimental, proactive or world-class international marketers as shown below.

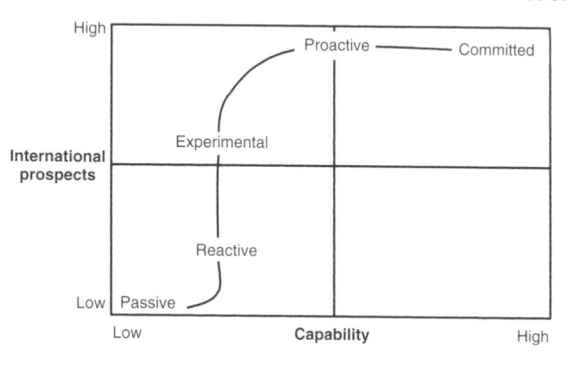

Fig. 6.3.

Source: Doole and Lowe: CIM Coursebook *Strategic Marketing Decisions* (Elsevier Butterworth-Heinemann, 2004)

Revision tips

■ There are strong drivers for globalisation resulting in pressure on organizations to operate internationally in some way.

■ Recognising the challenges in doing so, organizations have to make a fundamental strategic decision as to whether or not to adopt an international strategy.

■ In addition to economies of scale, there are many other benefits of operating internationally. An important benefit is being able to leverage both capability and corporate learning across global markets.

■ A range of international opportunities has been opened up for SMEs by, in particular, the Internet. In order to take advantage of these, SMEs have to develop and sustain niche markets.

INNOVATIVE STRATEGIES FOR FAST GLOBAL GROWTH

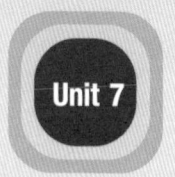

Unit 7

Entrepreneurial and hypergrowth businesses

- This unit examines the strategies developed by firms that have successfully met the challenges of achieving above average performance discussed in Units 2 and 3.

- Hypergrowth businesses are those businesses that have grown at more than 100% over the last 3 years. This unit discusses how this may be achieved.

- Organizations may be classified along a spectrum as Pioneers, Second-in, Imitators or Defensive Firms according to their attitude to innovation.

KEY DEFINITIONS

Assets – are the 'things' that the organization possesses, including the physical facilities, the customer database and brand.

Competencies – are skills that exist within the organization's staff, including brand management, IT and supply chain.

Core competencies – are the skills that pervade the organization and are those areas and activities in which the firm has a very high-developed ability.

Competitive advantage

Wilson and Gilligan (2004) suggest above average performance may be achieved by giving customers exceptional value.

Product differentiation advantages	Cost advantages
○ Superior quality	○ Consistent investment in R&D
○ Superior levels of service	○ High levels of process technology and production efficiency
○ Strong brand names	○ Patents
○ High levels of brand loyalty	○ Access to scarce or low cost resources
○ Distribution strengths	○ Vertical integration
○ High cost to the customer of switching	○ Distribution efficiency

Fig. 7.1.

Implementation – the drivers of entrepreneurial companies

Strategic Decisions relating to resource allocation in mature markets have to be made:

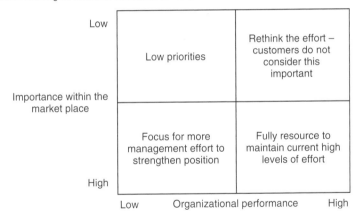

Fig. 7.2.
Source: Doole and Lowe: CIM Coursebook *Strategic Marketing Decisions* (Elsevier Butterworth-Heinemann, 2006)

Fast growth businesses

Fast growth businesses focus on high levels of **customer management**:

- Segmentation and sub-segmentation
- Understanding lifetime value of customers
- Exploiting cross-selling opportunities
- Managing customers through the whole buying process
- Building relationships with all stakeholders that influence decisions
- Focusing on providing the highest levels of service.

The **characteristics** of hypergrowth businesses are that they:

- Focus on being unique and offering exceptional customer value
- Define and exploit a defensible niche
- Have 'leading edge' products and services
- Lead in competitor and performance benchmarking
- Compete in areas that require speed, flexibility and exceptional customer service
- Diversify into related products and adjacent markets
- Leave the industry before the window of opportunity closes.

Beyond customer led: taking customers in a new direction identifying new market opportunity

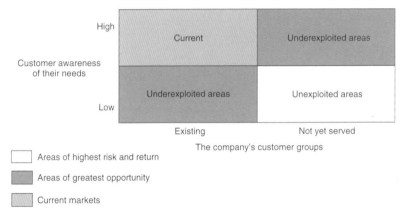

Fig. 7.3.
Source: Doole and Lowe: CIM Coursebook *Strategic Marketing Decisions* (Elsevier Butterworth-Heinemann, 2006)

E-business

E-business has become an important element in achieving fast growth for all companies and has enabled many small companies to reach larger markets than they would have otherwise done.

Chaffey *et al.* suggest four Internet business models:

1. Business to Business (B2B)
2. Business to Consumer (B2C)
3. Consumer to Consumer (C2C)
4. Consumer to Business (C2B)

In reality, the last of these is a model by which consumers form buying consortia to purchase from businesses.

Doole and Lowe suggest four categories of website:

- To provide organization information (e.g. www.philips.com)
- Site to provide service online (e.g. www.fedex.com)
- Site to provide information online (e.g. www.bbc.com)
- Site to carry out business transactions (e.g. www.expedia.co.uk)

Revision tips

- In order for organizations to achieve fast growth, suitable market opportunities for fast growth must be available in an industry, market conditions must be conducive to fast growth and the organization must have the necessary assets and competencies to take advantage of the situation.

- The availability of the Internet has created more fast growth opportunities and also brought about more conducive market conditions.

- In order to achieve fast growth, the organization's competencies are likely to include a dynamic and entrepreneurial approach to management.

- Having embarked on fast growth strategies, organizations must focus on effective management of their product and service portfolio taking particular note of competitor strategies, in order to sustain that growth.

- Because fast growth strategies tend to focus on changes in market conditions, which may also be identified by competitors, fast growth strategies are inherently high risk.

BUILDING PORTFOLIO VALUE: BRANDING, PRODUCTS AND SERVICES

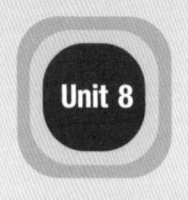

Products and brands

This unit addresses two important topic areas. The first is the management of an organization's portfolio of products through their lifecycle and the lifecycle of the markets that they serve. This will involve the building and maintenance of the portfolio, including rationalisation, where necessary, and the enhancement of products with added value services.

The second topic is that of branding. Brands are intangible assets which create value for both organizations and their customers. As with products, they must be carefully managed in order to leverage their value and avoid erosion of that value.

KEY DEFINITIONS

A successful brand – is an identifiable product, service or place augmented in such a way that the buyer or user perceives relevant, unique, sustainable added values that match their needs most closely (de Chematony, 2001).

Product portfolio – is the collection of products and services that are managed together rather than as individual products.

Brand equity – is the net present value of the future cash flow attributable to the brand name.

Intangible assets – non-material assets such as technical expertise, brands or patents.

Brands

Customer brand perception

Formed by:

- **Experience** of previous use
- **Personal referral** from friends and so on. Also **peer pressure**.
- **Editorial** and other public sources
- **Communications** by the organization, both through promotion and staff/customer interaction

Note also the Country of Origin (COO) effect, which, when used correctly, creates trust in the brand.

Categories of brands

Categorised by Doyle (2000) as:

- **Attribute brands** which build customer confidence through functional attributes.
- **Aspirational brands** that convey to customers images about the type of people who purchase the brand, so delivering status, recognition and esteem.
- **Experience brands** which focus on shared philosophy between customer and brand.

Brands

Benefits to the organization

Brands can add value to an organization by providing the following benefits (Doyle, 2000):

- Price premium
- Higher volumes
- Lower costs
- Better asset utilisation

Brand value erosion

The following factors can lead to the erosion of brand value:

- Private branding
- Brand forgery
- Negative brand associations
- Unacceptable business practices
- Unexpected crises
- Grey marketing

New product and service development

New products and services may fall into a number of categories, as shown opposite. It is important that decisions to commit time and resources to new developments are made in the context of the marketing strategy. In this respect, the questions on the following page need to be answered.

Table 8.1.

Category	Contribution
New to the world	10%
New product lines	20%
Additions to product lines	26%
Revisions/improvements	26%
Cost reductions	11%
Repositionings	7%

New product and service development

Aligning NPD to the marketing strategy

Table 8.2.

Fit with mission	Will all stakeholders understand the new idea?
Fit with product/market scope	Can the ideas be contained within an identified and easily communicated area?
Match between growth strategies and resources	Are the resources being used effectively within the growth options?
Delivery of competitive advantage	Is the advantage tangible or in the mind of the innovator?
Synergy between firm and target market	Will this add value to the current customer segment?
Fit with positioning	Does this reinforce or enhance the current positioning? Does it fit with the brand image?
Market entry alternatives	Could the idea be better exploited by alternative collaboration in order to reduce risks?
Is the timing right?	Should the product be launched now or should the firm wait for others to create the demand?

Revision tips

- The review of an organization's product and service portfolio involves a number of the most important strategic decisions that the organization will make. Products and services should not be viewed in isolation but in the context of the whole portfolio and the organization's business and marketing strategies.

- In an international and global environment, markets may be at different stages of their lifecycles and, for this and other reasons, products and services may be varied from market to market.

- Organizations gain significant value, often intangible and not shown on the balance sheet, from brands.

- Brands have great value in the B2 and NFP sectors as well as the B2C sector.

- There are a number of ways in which brands may be valued. One of these is to base the valuation on the net present value of future cashflows attributable to the brand name.

- Brands should be managed through their lifecycle, paying particular attention to the brand naming strategy (referred to as 'Brand Form' by some writers) and strategies, including innovation and promotion, to build, reposition and extend brands. It may also be necessary to rationalise brands from time to time.

- The challenge for global brands is to maintain consistency, where possible through standardisation, whilst adapting the mix to local conditions.

INTEGRATED COMMUNICATIONS AND RELATIONSHIP DEVELOPMENT

Unit 9

The role and purpose of communications

An organization can achieve competitive advantage by dint of the quality of its relationship with its stakeholders and an integrated strategy for communications is an important aspect of doing so. This unit deals with:

■ The purpose of communications in presenting and exchanging appropriate messages with stakeholders in a way that is integrated across the organization.

■ The role of communications in building and supporting relationships with an organization's stakeholders.

KEY DEFINITIONS

Integrated Marketing Communications – Shimp (2003) provides a definition of IMC which focuses on five features:

1. Start with the customer or prospect.
2. Use any form of relevant contact.
3. Achieve synergy through consistency across the communication elements.
4. Build relationships.
5. Affect behaviour.

Relationship marketing – is creating and building mutually beneficial relationships by bringing together the necessary stakeholders and resources to deliver the best possible perceived value proposition for the customer.

Internal, interactive and external marketing

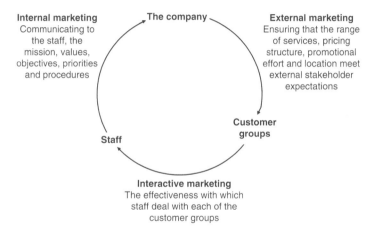

Internal marketing
Communicating to
the staff, the
mission, values,
objectives, priorities
and procedures

The company

External marketing
Ensuring that the range
of services, pricing
structure, promotional
effort and location meet
external stakeholder
expectations

**Customer
groups**

Staff

Interactive marketing
The effectiveness with which
staff deal with each of the
customer groups

Fig. 9.1.
Source: Doole and Lowe: CIM Coursebook *Strategic Marketing Decisions* (Elsevier Butterworth-Heinemann, 2006)

Four levels of communications and relationship building

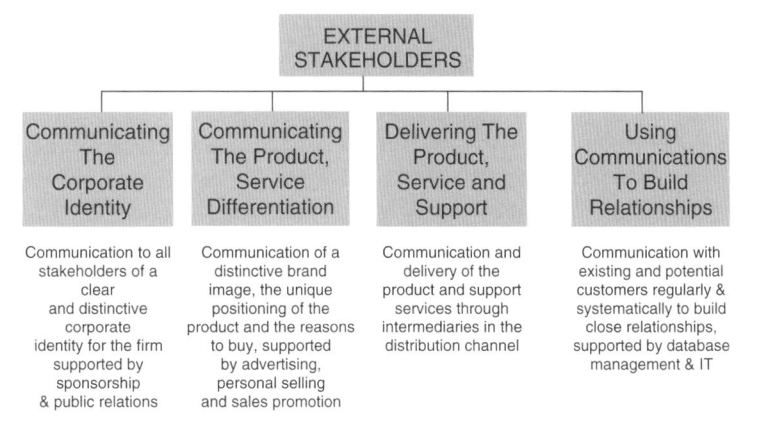

Fig. 9.2.
Source: Doole and Lowe: CIM Coursebook *Strategic Marketing Decisions* (Elsevier Butterworth-Heinemann, 2006)

The integration of communications

An organization communicates in eight ways (Davidson (2002)):

1. Actions
2. Behaviour
3. Face-to-face by management
4. Signals, from the organization's actions, facilities and objects
5. Product and services, especially their quality levels
6. Intended communications
7. Word of mouth and mouse
8. Comment by other organizations

The areas of integration

Corporate Strategy for internal and external stakeholders. Values, culture, policies, objectives, standards and style.

Brand Strategies for customers. Consistent messages to communicate what the brand stands for.

Global Integration. Whilst consistency of communications is essential and standardisation is desirable, there are pitfalls in over-standardisation.

Marketing Mix Integration. Customers receive communications from every element of the marketing mix, both intended and unintended.

Barriers to effective communications

Within the organization's control:

- Inconsistency in the messages conveyed to customers by staff at different levels, in different locations
- Different styles of presentation of corporate identity, brand and product image
- A lack of co-ordination of messages
- Failure to appreciate the differences in the fields of perception of the sender and receiver
- Ignoring the needs of different audiences
- Achieving little impact from a single message
- Lack of synergy and reinforcement from multiple communications
- More than one message communicated together, so confusing the recipient
- Setting unclear objectives
- Trying to achieve too much with one communication to justify the high cost
- Inconsistency within the distribution channel
- Advertising agencies focusing on their creative work rather than selling the product.

Problems outside the organization's control include:

- Counterfeiting or other infringements of patents
- Grey marketing, which is distribution through channels that are not authorised by the organization
- Competitors, governments or pressure groups attack the standards and values of organizations by alleging, fairly or unfairly, bad business practice.

Marketing communications planning

The marketing communications plan

Table 9.1.

Situation analysis	Environment market: stakeholders, competition, customers, structure
Objectives	The short- and long-term objectives
Messages	Target audiences and messages
Communications	The media, the promotions mix and integration of the channels
Budgets	Basis of allocation
Control	Measurement, evaluation and correct deviations

The B2b buying centre

Table 9.2.

Users	Often initiate the purchase and define the specification
Influences	Help define the product and evaluate the alternatives
Deciders	Decide product requirements and suppliers
Approvers	Authorise the proposals of deciders and buyers
Buyers	Have the formal authority for selecting suppliers and negotiating terms
Gatekeepers	Can stop the sellers reaching the buying centre

Communication tools and media

Media – Terminology

Reach is the percentage of the target audience exposed to the message at least once during the relevant period.

Coverage is the size of the potential audience that might be exposed to a potential medium.

Frequency is the repetition level of the communication.

Gross Rating Point (GRP) is the reach multiplied by the frequency and is a measure of the total number of exposures.

Efficiency is reaching as many customers as possible given a constant budget.

Recency as a concept suggests that potential customers must be reached when they are ready to buy.

The Communications Tools

Advertising is a one-way communication whose role can be to inform, persuade, remind and reinforce.

Sales promotion is a short-term means of increasing sales.

PR is perceived as 'news' and so more credible than advertising. A key role is in managing crises. **Sponsorship** is also a form of PR.

Personal selling is a two-way means of communication used when complex negotiations and persuasion are needed.

Direct marketing is a means of communication that tries to elicit a response from the customer. This is increasingly becoming a key part of a Relationship marketing strategy.

Relationship marketing – objectives

Relationship Marketing focuses on increasing the lifetime value of a customer and the following objectives:

- Maintain and build customers by offering more tailored and cost-effective business solutions

- Use existing relationships to obtain referral to other business units and supply chain members

- Increase the revenue from customers by offering solutions that are a combination of products and services

- Reduce the operational and communications cost of servicing the customers, including the work prior to a trading relationship.

Revision tips

■ Communication strategies must be integrated with each other, offering consistent messages to all stakeholders, and must also be consistent with the objectives and strategies of the organization.

■ Always consider who the audiences are and how they may be segmented. A stakeholder analysis will allow audiences to be identified in a particular situation.

■ Internal staff and staff in the extended organization are stakeholders and should be considered in any strategic communications decisions.

■ Relationship marketing includes the development of a Customer Relationship Management strategy that will involve integrating all aspects of marketing activity to build mutually beneficial relationships between customers, suppliers and other stakeholders.

USING THE EXTENDED ORGANIZATION TO ADD PORTFOLIO VALUE

Unit 10

LEARNING OUTCOMES

4.7 Examine the role of alliances and the creation of competitive advantage through supply chain development and marketing partnerships.

4.8 Examine how pricing policies and strategies can be used to build competitive advantage.

4.9 Explain the strategic management of the global portfolio and the expanded marketing mix.

Syllabus References: 4.7–4.9

The extended organization

■ This unit deals with two main topics. The first is the concept of the Extended Organization – the linked Value Chains at which level the customer buys. These linked Value Chains comprise both an organization's own value chain and that of its partners – suppliers and outsourced agencies.

■ The second topic is the nature of pricing, its objectives and strategies and its relationship to the cost drivers identified by the Value Chain Analysis.

KEY DEFINITIONS

The value chain – is the series of activities that create additional value for customers and comprises the use of materials, tangible and intangible assets.

A strategic alliance – is an informal arrangement between two or more organizations to pursue a common objective.

A joint venture – is a separate enterprise created using assets from two or more companies who share the equity and risk.

Porter's value chain

Michael Porter's Value Chain identifies the following primary and supporting activities that comprise the operating model of a simple, production-biased firm. These will differ significantly in other types of firm.

Primary Activities:

■ Inbound Logistics

■ Operations

■ Outbound Logistics

■ Marketing and Sales

■ Service

Secondary Activities:

■ The firm's infrastructure

■ Human resources management

■ Technology development

■ Procurement

Doyle (2000) explains the contributions that marketing makes to adding value and helping firms grow through:

■ Reducing costs through eliminating duplication and unnecessary processes

■ Benefiting from concentrating expertise and complementary activity

■ Exploiting new market opportunities

■ Reducing investment for organizations through outsourcing rather than manufacturing components

■ Enabling small firms to have similar costs to large firms.

Distribution channel management

Who best to supply the customer?

Table 10.1.

Manufacturer best placed to supply	Intermediaries best placed to supply
<ul><li>Complex products with continuous development</li><li>Made-to-order products</li><li>Where a high level of service and support is required</li><li>Where there is a small customer base</li><li>Where the transactions are of high volume or value</li><li>Easy to cover locations</li><li>Where shipments are large scale, planned and just-in-time</li><li>High level feedback is required</li></ul>	<ul><li>Simple product with basic service levels</li><li>Standard stocked lines</li><li>Large customer base</li><li>Smaller customers</li><li>Geographically difficult to cover</li><li>Small random deliveries from stock</li><li>Low level feedback</li></ul>

Routes to market

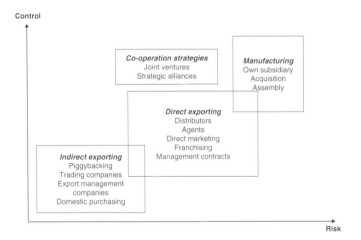

Fig. 10.1.
Source: Doole and Lowe: CIM Coursebook *Strategic Marketing Decisions* (Elsevier Butterworth-Heinemann, 2004)

Pricing decisions

Table 10.2.

- Survival
- Return on investment
- Market stabilisation
- Maintenance and improvement of position
- Reflecting product differentiation
- Market skimming
- Market penetration
- Early cash recovery
- Preventing new entry

In responding to price-based competition, organizations should consider the following:

■ Whether they are a leader, follower or me too

■ Whether they can prevent new entry

■ Whether their cost levels offer scope for price cutting

■ Whether they, or their competitors, have the resources for a price war

■ Whether they are dependent on the product

■ Whether they are committed to the market sector

■ The potential returns from price cutting

■ The distinctiveness of the product and brand loyalty

■ Whether a price cut will affect the perception of brand value

Portfolio integration decisions

Table 10.3. Portfolio integration

	Providing opportunity to increase prices (or revenue)	Making cost reductions to increase revenue or profitability
Product portfolio		Better sourcing
		Better plant utilisation
		Better use of raw materials and labour
		Design or specification changes
Service enhancement		Better use of labour and processes
		Better use of assets (yield management)
Promotion		Better choice of communication methods from mix elements
		More targeted, less mass communications
Channel		More value from channel
	Reintermediation	Disintermediation
Relationship		Cost effective one-2-one marketing
	Value chain contribution	Supply-chain efficiency

Source: Doole and Lowe: CIM Coursebook *Strategic Marketing Decisions* (Elsevier Butterworth-Heinemann, 2006)

Revision tips

■ Remember that channels have a variety of roles and, while disintermediation through using the Internet can save costs there may be a consequent loss of channel functions and, therefore, a reduction in customer service levels.

■ The Value Chain is a useful tool for identifying where an organization can add value or save cost. It will, however, be different for different types of organizations and, in particular, will comprise of primary functions specific to those types of organization.

■ Linkages between elements of the Value Chain, and the effectiveness of links to the Value Chains of other organizations are important because customers typically buy at the level of the *linked* Value Chains.

■ In making strategic pricing decisions, it is extremely important to know what factors affect a firm's reaction in the face of a pricing attack. The firm must understand its own objectives, strategies, strengths and weaknesses as well as those of its competitors. It may then decide to maintain or drop prices or, possibly, withdraw from the market altogether.

FINANCIAL APPRAISAL
FOR STRATEGIC MARKETING
DECISIONS

Unit 11

LEARNING OUTCOMES

5.1 Examine the implications of strategic marketing decisions for implementation and control.

5.3 Apply investment appraisal techniques to marketing investment decisions.

5.4 Examine alternative approaches to modelling potential investment decisions in the deployment of marketing resources.

5.6 Define budgetary and planning control techniques for use in the control of marketing plans and explain the pitfalls of control systems and how they may be overcome.

Syllabus References: 5.1, 5.3, 5.4, 5.6

Financial measures

■ The ultimate measure of the value of any activity is financial. However, this financial return may be neither immediate nor direct. Ways of measuring the true value of this return must be found in order to justify it.

■ In this unit the way in which added value to a company is measured are considered. Three approaches are evaluated: Cashflow, Economic Value Added (EVA) and Return on Capital Employed (ROCE).

■ In addition, both Cost/Volume/Profit (Breakeven) analysis as a means of supporting short term decisions and ratio analysis, as a measure of performance, are considered.

Return on capital employed – is a measure commonly used by companies to assess the added value to shareholders resulting from the capital invested.

Payback – measures the number of years it will take to recover the original investment from the net cash flows resulting from a project. The method is based on being able to estimate a future flow of funds.

Cost/Volume/Profit (CVP) analysis – is used to help a company understand the relationship between volume, costs and profits and used to budget and forecast the break-even point.

A ratio – takes two variables (e.g. profit/sales) and compares them with other measures of the same variable in another time period or in another company in order to assess the performance of the company and the efficiency of its operations.

Financial analysis for long-term decision making

Investment projects may be evaluated on a number of bases. These include Payback Period and Net Present Value.

The objective of Payback Period is simply to determine how long it will take to recover the investment made from the net profit on that investment.

The objective of the second is to take into account the 'time value of money' in evaluating the investment. The exact timing of the return is required and a Discount Rate (usually given from tables although it is simple to calculate) is applied to each year's net income, resulting in that amount being reduced to reflect the fact that money received in the future is worth less than money received now and so immediately available for reinvestment.

Payback Period

$$\text{No. of years} = \frac{\text{Total Investment}}{\text{Net income per year}}$$

Note that the income may vary each year and so a calculation of the cumulative net income will be required to determine the exact time at which the investment is recovered.

Net Present Value

The Net Present Value of an income stream is calculated as:

(Income year 1) × (Year 1 Discount Rate)
+ (Income year 2) × (Year 2 Discount Rate)
+ (Income year 3) × (Year 3 Discount Rate) etc.

Now the initial investment can be evaluated depending on whether it is less (☺) or more (☹) than the NPV of the above income stream.

Assessing owner/shareholder value

One of the main objectives of business is to maximise shareholders' wealth by adding value to the company or organization. Three methods of measuring this Shareholder Added Value are considered.

Cashflow Valuation

The calculation of cashflow generated by a strategy can be split into two parts:

1. Present Value (PV) of Cashflow during the forecast period. Calculated as the PV of the net cashflows (income less expenditure) during the forecast period.

2. PV of Cashflow after the period (residual value).

The latter is difficult to attribute to marketing strategies and so they may often be evaluated on the basis of the first alone.

Economic Value Added

This is simply the amount by which the return on an investment exceeds the cost of the capital required for that investment.

EVA = Net Operating Profits After Tax

- (capital invested
× weighted average cost of that capital)

The figure in brackets is effectively the return that could have been secured by investing that capital elsewhere.

Return on Capital Employed (ROCE)

$$ROCE = \frac{\text{Earnings Before Interest \& Tax}^* \ 100\%}{\text{Capital Employed}}$$

Doyle is critical of this measure because the value of earnings (which includes the value of assets) may be arbitrary and subject to risk.

Cost/volume/profit (CVP) analysis

One of the main functions of CVP Analysis is to enable the Breakeven Point for a product (or range of products) to be calculated. This is the point at which the volume is such that neither a profit nor a loss is being made on that product. Above this volume a profit will be made; below it, a loss will be suffered.

$$\text{Breakeven Volume} = \frac{\text{Total Fixed Costs}}{\text{Contribution per unit}}$$

In order to calculate the volume required to make a given level of profit, that profit may be considered as an additional fixed cost. So:

$$\text{Vol required for profit of £NN} = \frac{\text{Total Fixed Costs} + \text{NN}}{\text{Contribution per unit}}$$

CVP Analysis Definitions	
Fixed Costs:	Costs that do not vary with production volume
Variable Costs:	Costs that do vary with production volume
Contribution per unit:	Sales Revenue per unit minus Variable Costs per unit
Margin of safety %:	The percentage by which sales would have to fall before a loss is made. A measure of risk.
Contribution Sales Ratio	$\dfrac{\text{Selling Price} - \text{Variable Cost}}{\text{Selling Price}}$
Profit Volume Ratio:	$\dfrac{\text{Sales Revenue} - \text{Total Variable Costs}}{\text{Sales Revenue}}$

Financial techniques for evaluating performance

Ratio analysis is useful for showing trends over a period of time and for enabling companies to compare their performance with that of other companies in similar industries.

Profitability Ratios

Gross Profit Margin $\dfrac{\text{Gross Profit} \times 100\%}{\text{Sales Turnover}}$

Net Profit Margin $\dfrac{\text{Net Profit} \times 100\%}{\text{Sales Turnover}}$

Sales Ratios

Stock Turnover $\dfrac{\text{Annual Cost of Goods Sold}}{\text{Average Stock Value}}$

NB: This figure is expressed as a no. of times/year

Operational Ratios

Current Ratio: Current assets : Current liabilities

Quick Ratio: (Current assets − Stock) : Current Liabilities

Debt Collection Period: $\dfrac{\text{Debtors}}{\text{Credit sales}/365}$

Creditor Payment Period: $\dfrac{\text{Creditors}}{\text{CreditPurchases}/365}$

Revision tips

- Investment Decisions relate to the comparison of an investment (often initial) to the income or savings accruing as a result of that investment over a period of time. The comparison may be done on a payback, NPV or, possibly, an accounting rate of return basis. If you are asked to calculate the PV of an income and/or an expenditure stream, you will be given the discount factors which should simply be applied to the figures for the appropriate year.

- Investments in individual marketing campaigns may be evaluated on the same basis.

- Short-term decisions, typically at product or product group level, will be based on techniques such as Breakeven Analysis or Cost/Volume/Profit Analysis. Ensure that you are familiar with both.

- To track performance of decisions after they have been made, ratio analysis is an appropriate tool for identifying and tracking trends and also for making comparisons with similar organizations operating in the similar markets.

- Numerical questions represent an opportunity for relatively easy marks. Ensure that you study, and understand, the model answers in all previous exam papers.

ACHIEVING A SUSTAINABLE COMPETITIVE ADVANTAGE

Unit 12

LEARNING OUTCOMES

4.10 Assess the issues of corporate and social responsibility (CSR), sustainability and ethics in achieving competitive advantage, enhancing corporate reputation and creating stakeholder value.

5.2 Explain the concept of, and evaluate methods such as balanced scorecard for, stakeholder value measurement.

5.5 Define performance measurement systems for the deployment of marketing assets and the implementation of marketing plans.

5.6 Define budgetary and planning control techniques for use in the control of marketing plans and explain the pitfalls of control systems and how they may be overcome.

Syllabus References: 4.10, 5.2, 5.5, 5.6

Measuring performance

In order for an organization to make effective decisions, the contribution of strategic marketing decisions themselves must be capable of being demonstrated to be effective. This unit addresses:

- ■ The approaches a manager can take to develop efficient and effective control systems
- ■ The development of a process through which stakeholder value can be measured
- ■ The process by which the performance of a marketing program can be critically evaluated
- ■ The issues and role of Corporate Social Responsibility in sustaining competitive advantage and creating shareholder value by enhancing reputation.

KEY DEFINITIONS

Evaluation and control mechanisms – set standards to which marketing strategies should aspire, measure performance and take corrective action when the measurement varies from the level of performance required.

The Balanced Scorecard – is a management system to measure current performance and to set priorities for future performance. It incorporates four perspectives: financial perspective, the customer perspective, the internal business perspective and the innovation and learning perspective.

Corporate social responsibility – is the term used to describe the level of awareness shown by companies of their social responsibility and the values exhibited with regard to the societal impact of strategic marketing decisions.

Approaches to measuring performance

In order for marketing to be properly represented at board level, its contribution to profitability and shareholder value must be capable of being demonstrated. This is done by establishing sound control systems and performance metrics.

Objectives of Control Systems

- To set standards to which marketing strategies should aspire
- To measure performance in a meaningful way
- To assess areas of strengths and weaknesses in marketing programmes
- To establish mechanisms for taking corrective action when required

Performance Metrics

- **What** are they going to measure
- What are the **organizational mechanisms** for the measuring activities:
  - Benchmarking
  - Annual Budgeting procedures
  - Auditing
- How to ensure performance is measured against **a balanced range of goals and objectives**, for example, those of the balanced scorecard:
  - Financial
  - Customers
  - Internal Business
  - Innovation and Learning Perspective

Stakeholders

Stakeholders can be classified into six groups
(Doyle, 2000):

1. Shareholders/owners
2. Employees
3. Managers
4. Customers
5. Suppliers
6. Community and Society

Typical Stakeholders of a company

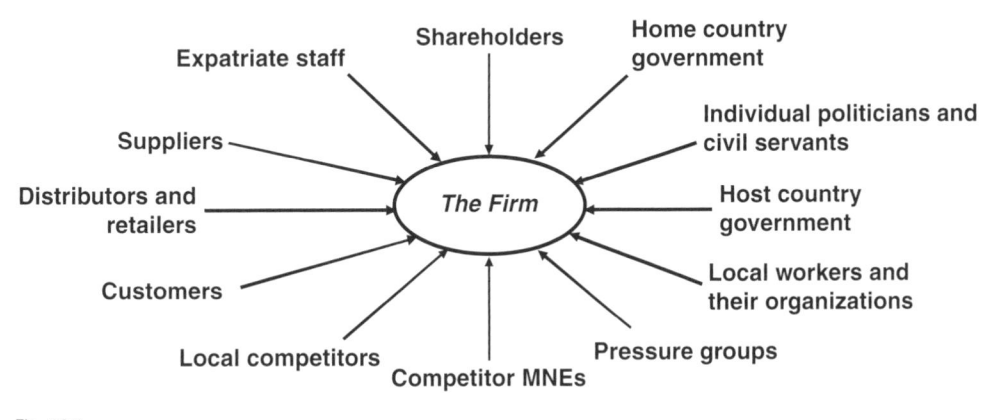

Fig. 12.1.

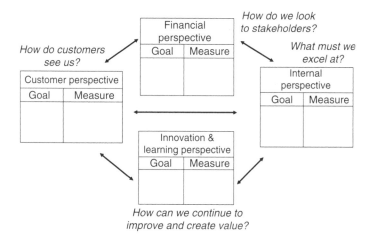

Fig. 12.2.

Ethics and corporate social responsibility

Many companies and professional bodies have codes of ethics and are also regulated by consumer watchdogs and ombudsmen as well as by law.

In addition, companies can differentiate themselves from competitors by dint of their position on Corporate Social Responsibility (CSR). Whilst some companies may simply react or take a defensive position on CSR, other have succeeded in building competitive advantage on a proactive positioning towards CSR by sharing the values of their stakeholders. The societal marketing concept is based on enhancing the well-being of society as well as that of the consumer and shareholders.

Revision tips

■ It is expected that Strategic Decisions will be subject to evaluation. The approach and processes that you recommend to this evaluation are an important element of strategic decision making.

■ In making Strategic Decisions, you should, therefore, consider both how they will be evaluated (in terms of process) and, equally importantly, the bases on which they will be evaluated.

■ Strategic Decisions may be evaluated on a strictly short-term basis. However, in order to demonstrate that they increase shareholder value, their implications in terms of improving, or putting in place the capabilities to improve, customer value should also be considered. Kaplan and Norton's Balanced Scorecard provides one mechanism to achieve this.

■ When considering the balanced scorecard, it is very important to recognise that each perspective has a causal relationship with the levels above it. Similarly, each level may rely on the success of initiatives in the levels below.

■ The ethical and CSR implications of Strategic Decisions should also be considered. In particular, an organization should understand clearly its stance on ethics and CSR, whether it be defensive or reactive, or whether it seeks to align itself with the values of its stakeholders and so achieve a competitive advantage in doing so. In the latter case, its mission, objectives, strategy and marketing programmes should be consistent with this stance.